Holistic feeding: the secret to healthy and happy pets!

By Gonzalo Estrada

HOLISTIC FEEDING

First edition. March 12, 2024.

Copyright © 2024 Gonzalo Estrada.

ISBN: 979-8224054862

Written by Gonzalo Estrada.

Table of Contents

Contents

Chapter 1: Introduction to Holistic Pet Food

Discover the basics of holistic feeding so you can provide a healthy and happy life for your pet.

Feeding our pets is a fundamental aspect of their well-being and happiness. Like us, they also require a balanced diet adapted to their specific needs. This is where holistic eating comes into play.

Holistic pet nutrition is based on the idea of treating the animal as a whole: body, mind and spirit. Instead of simply providing them with food that covers their basic nutritional needs, we seek to feed them in a more complete way and in tune with their nature.

But what does holistic eating really mean? In a nutshell, it's about feeding our pets naturally, using fresh, quality ingredients. Organic is prioritized, avoiding processed foods, artificial additives and by-products that do not provide real benefits to your body.

By opting for a holistic diet, we are promoting a healthy and balanced life for our beloved pets. This involves not only providing them with adequate food, but also taking into account aspects such as regular exercise, stress management and mental stimulation.

One of the key aspects of holistic nutrition is the choice of natural and fresh ingredients. We can include lean meat, vegetables and fruits, whole grains, and healthy oils in your diet. By doing so, we're providing them with the nutrients they need for their development and overall well-being.

It's important to remember that every pet is unique and has specific requirements. Not all animals have the same nutritional needs, so it is advisable to consult a veterinarian or animal feed specialist to determine the most appropriate diet for our pet.

Another aspect to consider is the amount of food we offer our pet. Finding the right balance is essential to avoid both malnutrition and overweight. A veterinarian will be able to guide the amount of food needed, taking into account the age, size, activity level and health status of our pet.

In addition to the right food choice, holistic eating also encompasses other aspects such as conscious eating and the way in which we relate to our pets during meals. It's important to set regular feeding times and avoid giving them leftovers from our food, as this can be detrimental to their long-term health.

In short, holistic pet food is one way to provide them with a healthy and happy life. By choosing fresh and natural ingredients, providing them with a balanced diet and considering other important aspects, such as exercise and mental stimulation, we will be promoting their overall well-being.

Remember, the most important thing is to be attentive to the individual needs of our pets and adapt their diet according to them. In the second part of this chapter, we will further explore the benefits of holistic feeding and some practical tips for implementing it in the daily lives of our pets.

Don't miss it!

*It will continue*In this second part of the chapter, we'll continue to explore the benefits of holistic pet food and give you some practical tips to implement it into your furry companion's daily life.

A key benefit of holistic feeding is the positive impact it has on the health and well-being of our pets. By providing them with fresh, natural food, we're making sure they get the essential nutrients they need to stay strong and healthy. A balanced diet with quality ingredients will strengthen your immune system, promote gut health and help prevent common pet diseases, such as obesity, diabetes and heart disease.

In addition, holistic feeding can also contribute to improving the emotional health of our pets. Feeding them mindfully and setting regular meal times gives them a sense of security and stability. This can be especially beneficial for those animals that have experienced traumatic situations or are suffering from anxiety. Food becomes a moment of connection and gratification, strengthening the bond between you and your pet.

Now, let's get to the practical tips! The first thing is to make sure you're choosing quality, fresh ingredients for your pet's diet. Consider incorporating lean meat, such as chicken or fish, vegetables and fruits such as carrots or apples, whole grains such as brown rice, and healthy oils such as salmon oil. Always consider your pet's specific needs and consult a veterinarian before making any dietary changes.

Another important aspect is the amount of food you provide to your pet. Finding the right balance is essential to avoid weight problems, both malnutrition and being overweight can be harmful to your health. Your veterinarian will be the best person to advise you on the appropriate amount of food, taking into account their age, size, activity level and health status.

In addition to food choices, we must also pay attention to how we relate to our pets during meals. Don't forget to set regular times to feed them and avoid giving them leftovers from our food, as this can alter their balanced diet and lead to digestive or health problems in the long term. Reserve a quiet, distraction-free space so they can enjoy their meal in a relaxed way.

Always remember to keep your pet's individual needs in mind! Every animal is unique and what works for one may not be right for another. Watch your pet closely, pay attention to their behavior and mood, and adjust their diet as needed. Being attentive to the signals your furry companion gives you is key to ensuring their well-being and happiness.

In conclusion, holistic feeding for pets is much more than simply providing them with food. It's a way of life that seeks to promote your overall health and happiness. By opting for a holistic approach, we are giving our pets an opportunity to live healthier, fuller lives.

We hope this chapter has been helpful in understanding the basics of holistic pet nutrition and how to implement it in your furry companion's daily life. In the next chapter, we'll further explore the different holistic feeding options available on the market and how to choose the best one for your pet. Don't miss it!

Keep reading and you'll discover more tips and recommendations to provide your pet with a holistic and satisfying diet. See you soon!

Chapter 2: Benefits of Holistic Eating

Explore the many benefits that a holistic diet can provide to your pet, from better gut health to a shiny coat.

When it comes to ensuring a healthy and happy life for our pets, there's no doubt that food plays a fundamental role. Like us, they also deserve a balanced and nutritious diet that meets all their needs. This is where holistic nutrition stands out, as an option that seeks the total well-being of our beloved furry companions.

First, holistic feeding focuses on providing our pets with quality, natural nutrition. This involves using fresh, minimally processed ingredients, avoiding artificial additives and low-quality by-products that could compromise your health. By nourishing our friends with natural, high-quality food, we are providing a strong foundation for their overall well-being.

One of the most notable benefits of a holistic diet is the positive impact it has on the digestive system of pets. By eliminating artificial and processed ingredients that can wreak havoc on your intestinal system, we promote optimal digestive health. This translates into greater absorption of nutrients, reduction of digestive problems and significant relief in cases of food sensitivities or intolerances.

In addition, a holistic diet can help maintain the proper weight of our pets. By focusing on natural ingredients and limiting the use of refined carbohydrates, the risk of overweight and obesity is reduced. A pet at a healthy weight will benefit from greater energy, better mobility, and a lower incidence of weight-related diseases.

Another important aspect of holistic nutrition is its impact on the health of our pets' skin and coat. By using natural and quality ingredients, the necessary nutrients are provided to maintain healthy skin, a shiny coat and free from problems such as dryness, dandruff or irritation. A holistic diet rich in essential fatty acids and antioxidants will help your pet to look radiant.

In addition, holistic nutrition strengthens the immune system of our pets. Natural and fresh foods contain vitamins, minerals and antioxidants that help strengthen the body's defenses. A pet with a robust immune system is less likely to contract diseases and infections, and has a greater ability to fight and recover from illness.

Last but not least, holistic feeding can have a significant impact on the behavior and mental health of our pets. The quality of the food they eat is directly related to their emotional well-being and energy level. By providing them with a balanced and nutritious diet, we are promoting a positive mood, greater concentration and greater overall vitality.

In conclusion, holistic feeding offers a wide range of benefits for our pets. From improving gut health to maintaining a radiant coat, this way of eating is based on natural, quality ingredients that promote total well-being. By choosing a holistic diet, we are investing in the health and happiness of our beloved pets.

The second half of this chapter will focus on the additional benefits that holistic feeding can offer our pets. We will continue to explore how this way of eating can positively impact your overall health and well-being.

Another important benefit of holistic eating is its effect on the dental health of our pets. By providing them with natural, quality food, we are promoting dental cleaning and preventing the accumulation of plaque and tartar. Processed foods and artificial treats can cause dental problems, such as periodontal disease and bad breath. However, with a holistic diet rich in natural ingredients, our pets can maintain a healthy smile and fresh breath.

In addition to the physical benefits, holistic feeding can also have an impact on the emotional well-being of our pets. Many studies have shown that a balanced, nutrient-rich diet can positively affect the mood of animals. By providing them with natural, quality food, we're providing our pets with the nutrients they need to maintain a proper chemical balance in their brain, which can help reduce stress, anxiety and improve their overall mental health.

In addition, by avoiding artificial ingredients and food additives, we are reducing the risk of allergies and food sensitivities in our pets. Many processed foods may contain ingredients that cause allergic reactions in animals, such as itchy skin, irritation, digestive problems, etc. However, with a holistic diet based on natural and fresh ingredients, we are minimizing the risk of allergies and promoting better overall health.

Holistic feeding can also have an impact on the longevity of our pets. By providing them with a balanced and nutritious diet from an early age, we are laying the foundation for a healthy and long life. Pets that feed holistically have a greater chance of living longer and aging healthier, avoiding age-related diseases and maintaining a high level of energy throughout their lives.

Last but not least, holistic eating can help prevent chronic diseases in our pets. By providing them with a rich variety of natural foods, we are providing their bodies with the essential nutrients they need to function properly and strengthen their immune system. A pet with a strong immune system is less likely to develop chronic diseases, such as diabetes, heart disease and respiratory problems, among others.

In short, holistic feeding offers a wide range of benefits for our pets. From maintaining a healthy smile to improving mental well-being and preventing chronic diseases, this way of eating is based on natural, quality ingredients that promote a healthy and happy lifestyle for our beloved pets. By choosing a holistic diet, we are investing in the health and well-being of our furry companions, ensuring that they have a long and healthy life by our side.

Chapter 3: The Importance of Natural Ingredients

In today's world, more and more people are recognizing the benefits of living a healthy and balanced lifestyle. And not only do we, human beings, benefit from choosing natural and nutritious foods, but also our beloved pets can get a healthier and happier life if we provide them with a holistic diet, based on natural ingredients.

But what exactly are natural ingredients and why are they essential in feeding our pets? Natural ingredients refer to those that come from natural sources, without the intervention of artificial chemicals or industrial processing. These ingredients are rich in essential nutrients and are easily digested, allowing our pets to take full advantage of their health benefits.

Choosing natural food for our pets is crucial, as artificial and processed ingredients can have a negative impact on their overall well-being. Some of these ingredients may include low-quality meat by-products, fillers, chemical additives and preservatives, all of which can lead to health problems such as allergies, obesity and chronic diseases.

By opting for a holistic diet based on natural ingredients, we are providing our pets with balanced nutrition that meets all their needs. These foods are made up of high-quality protein sources, such as lean meat, fish, and chicken, along with whole grains, fresh fruits and vegetables. These natural ingredients are full of vitamins, minerals and antioxidants that strengthen our pets' immune systems, promote healthy skin and a shiny coat, and improve digestive health.

In addition to nutritional benefits, holistic feeding based on natural ingredients can also have a positive impact on the behavior and energy of our pets. By avoiding artificial additives and preservatives, we can help prevent behavioral problems related to hyperactivity, lack of concentration and anxiety. Our pets will feel calmer and more balanced, which will be reflected in their daily lives.

Now that we understand the importance of natural ingredients in the holistic nutrition of our pets, the question arises: how to choose the right foods for our faithful companions? It's essential to read pet food labels carefully and look for those that contain high-quality, natural ingredients. Avoid those that have meat by-products, processed flours, and artificial chemicals on their ingredient list.

The best option is to choose foods that are certified organic, free of GMOs and raised without the use of hormones or antibiotics. These foods ensure that our pets are receiving the highest quality natural ingredients, with no compromises in terms of health and well-being.

In the next chapter, we'll dive deeper into the topic of how to select the right foods for your pet and share some practical tips to make holistic eating an essential part of their daily lives. Don't miss it!

Continued... Once we understand the importance of natural ingredients in the holistic feeding of our pets, it's time to learn how to select the right foods for them. Here are some practical tips to help you incorporate holistic eating into your faithful companion's daily life.

First, it's essential to know your pet's specific needs. Each animal is unique and requires a diet adapted to its age, size, activity level and health status. If you have any questions about what type of food is most suitable for your pet, do not hesitate to consult your veterinarian. They can recommend the best option based on the individual needs of your faithful friend.

Once you know what type of food is right for your pet, it's important to read food labels carefully to make sure they contain high-quality, natural ingredients. Look for those that are formulated with high-quality protein sources, such as lean meat, fish, and chicken. Avoid those that contain meat by-products, such as processed flours or low-quality by-products.

In addition to protein, it's important that pet food contains a variety of essential nutrients. Look for those that contain whole grains, fresh fruits and vegetables. These ingredients provide vitamins, minerals and antioxidants that strengthen your pet's immune system, promote healthy skin and a shiny coat, and improve digestive health.

Another thing to consider when choosing the right foods for your pet is to avoid artificial additives and preservatives. These ingredients can have a negative impact on your health and well-being. Choose foods that are free of artificial chemicals and preservatives, as this will help prevent behavioral problems related to hyperactivity, lack of concentration and anxiety in your pet.

In addition to choosing natural foods, you can also supplement your pet's diet with nutritional supplements. These supplements can help boost your pet's health and well-being, providing them with the additional nutrients they may need.

Always remember to consider your pet's individual needs when choosing the right foods. If you have any concerns or questions, don't hesitate to consult your veterinarian, as they can provide you with the best guidance to ensure that your pet is receiving adequate nutrition.

In short, holistic nutrition based on natural ingredients is essential to offer our pets a healthy and happy life. By choosing foods with high-quality natural ingredients, we are providing our pets with balanced nutrition that meets all their needs. This translates into benefits for their health and well-being, including a strengthened immune system, healthy skin and a shiny coat, and balanced behavior.

In addition, it's essential to remember that every pet is unique, and their needs may vary. Therefore, it is important to consult a veterinarian to receive personalized guidance on the right diet for your pet.

We hope these practical tips will help you incorporate holistic nutrition based on natural ingredients into your pet's daily life. Always remember to read food labels carefully and offer your faithful companion quality nutrition. Your pet will thank you with a healthier and happier life!

Chapter 4: The Power of Raw Food

L earn how including raw food in your pet's diet can improve their digestion, immune system and quality of life.

A healthy diet is essential for the well-being of our beloved pets. Like us, they also need a balanced and nutritious diet to enjoy a long and happy life. In this chapter, we'll explore the power of raw food and how it can benefit your furry companion in a holistic way.

Raw foods, also known as the BARF (Biologically Appropriate Raw Food) diet, are based on providing pets with a diet similar to what they would have in their natural state. They consist of raw and fresh ingredients, preserving to a greater extent the essential nutrients that can be lost during the cooking process.

One of the main benefits of feeding raw food is its effect on your pet's digestion. As they are not subjected to high temperatures, these foods retain the natural enzymes that help break down nutrients, making them easier to absorb by the body. In this way, cases of indigestion, gas and gastrointestinal problems are reduced, allowing your pet to enjoy adequate digestive function.

In addition, including raw food in your pet's diet strengthens their immune system. These foods are rich in vitamins, minerals and natural antioxidants, which help fight free radicals and strengthen the body's defenses. By providing your pet with a balanced diet full of nutrients, you'll be helping to prevent various diseases and keep them strong and healthy throughout their lives.

Another important aspect to consider is your pet's quality of life. Feeding raw food has been linked to a significant improvement in animals' vigor and energy. By providing them with a diet adapted to their needs, you will be promoting an active and vibrant lifestyle. Your pets will feel happier, more energetic and more willing to do activities they like, such as playing, running and exploring.

It is necessary to note that the transition to a raw food diet should be gradual and under the supervision of a veterinarian. Every pet is unique and may need different amounts and types of raw food. It's important to make sure they're getting all the nutrients they need to maintain their health and well-being.

In the next chapter, we will continue to further explore the benefits of raw food in feeding our pets. We will discover which ingredients are the most recommended, how to prepare balanced meals and what considerations we must take into account when making the switch to this diet.

Remember, a holistic diet, such as one based on raw foods, can make a difference in your pet's life. Don't miss the chance to provide them with the best food and care so they can enjoy a full and healthy life.

Keep reading in the next chapter and you'll discover how to put this transformation into practice! In addition to improving your pet's digestion, immune system and quality of life, including raw food in their diet can also have benefits in other important aspects of their health. Next, we'll explore some of these benefits and how you can implement a raw food-based diet in a practical and safe way for your beloved furry companion.

One of the reasons raw foods are so beneficial for pets is because they resemble the diet they would have in the wild. These foods contain an optimal amount of essential nutrients, such as high-quality protein, healthy fats, vitamins and minerals. By providing your pet with a more natural diet, you'll be helping to regulate their weight properly and keep their body in shape.

In addition, a raw food diet can be especially beneficial for pets with food allergies or intolerances. Many commercial foods contain ingredients that can trigger allergic reactions in some sensitive pets. By opting for raw food, you can better control the ingredients you consume and eliminate those that may cause health problems for your pet.

Another important aspect to consider is dental hygiene. Raw foods, such as raw bones and meat with bones, provide natural exercise for jaw muscles and help keep teeth clean and healthy. By chewing raw food, pets get rid of tartar and dental plaque, thus preventing periodontal disease and other oral problems.

Feeding raw food can also have a positive impact on your pet's mood and behavior. By providing them with a balanced, nutrient-packed diet, you'll be helping to keep their nervous system in good shape and improve their mental health. Many pet owners have reported a reduction in behavioral problems, such as aggression or anxiety, after switching to a raw food-based diet.

The transition to a raw food diet may seem daunting at first, but with a little planning and proper counseling, it's totally doable. The most important thing is to find a veterinarian who is familiar with this type of diet and can guide you through the transition process. This specialist will be able to design a personalized feeding plan for your pet, taking into account their individual nutritional needs and ensuring that they receive all the essential nutrients.

It's important to remember that feeding raw food isn't just about giving raw meat to pets. You need to include a variety of foods, such as fleshy bones, organs, fruits, and vegetables. These ingredients must be carefully selected and provided in the right proportions to ensure a balanced diet.

In addition, it is essential to follow strict hygiene and food safety guidelines when handling raw foods. Wash your hands with warm water and soap after handling them and make sure you clean the surfaces and kitchen utensils used properly.

In short, including raw food in your pet's diet can have positive effects on their overall health. From better digestion and immune system to greater vitality and mental well-being, raw food can make a big difference in the life of your furry companion. Don't hesitate to do more research and consult a veterinarian to begin the transition to a holistic and natural diet for your pet.

Remember, a responsible owner is willing to research and make changes to their pet's diet to ensure that they are receiving the best possible care. Read on and learn more about how to implement raw food into your pet's diet in the next chapter. Your pet will thank you!

Chapter 5: Holistic dog food

Learn specific guidelines to feed your dog holistically and ensure their overall well-being.

In today's world, where concern for health and well-being is growing, it's imperative that we apply the same principles to our pets. Dogs, our loyal companions, also benefit from a holistic diet that promotes their health and happiness.

Holistic dog food is based on the understanding that their well-being goes beyond simply providing them with a balanced diet. It involves understanding their individual needs and providing them with a nutritious and balanced diet, adapted to their age, size, race and health status.

The first step to feeding your dog holistically is to choose quality food. Opt for natural and organic options, without artificial colors, preservatives or low-quality by-products. Just like us, our dog's benefit from fresh, unprocessed ingredients. Look for trustworthy brands that offer balanced foods based on high-quality protein, healthy carbohydrates and essential fats.

The next important thing is to determine the right amount of food for your dog. While the instructions on the labels can serve as a reference, it's crucial to adjust them according to your pet's individual needs. Consider their activity level, age, size and metabolism. Observe your body and if necessary, consult your veterinarian for more precise guidance.

The frequency of meals should also be considered. Although there are different approaches, many experts recommend dividing the daily diet into two or three meals. This helps keep your dog from feeling hungry and keeps his metabolism active. Make sure to set a regular meal schedule and avoid feeding him leftovers from the table, as some human foods can be harmful to his health.

In addition to dry or canned food, consider including fresh food in your dog's diet. Vegetables such as carrots, broccoli, and squash can provide additional nutrients and boost your digestive health. Fruits such as apples and blueberries can also be enjoyed as healthy treats.

Remember that holistic eating isn't just about what you eat, it's also about how you eat. It provides a calm and distraction-free environment during your dog's meals. Avoid haste and allow him to chew his food properly. Some dogs may need special plates to eat more slowly to avoid digestive problems.

In this first half of the chapter, we have covered the basic guidelines for offering a holistic diet to your dog. From choosing quality foods to establishing a proper eating routine, these steps will help you promote your overall well-being. However, there is still more to discover and explore.

In the second half of this chapter, we'll invite you to explore natural diet options for dogs, discover how to incorporate dietary supplements, and learn about the benefits of a homemade diet. Don't miss your chance to take your dog's health to the next level! In the second half of this chapter, we'll continue to explore natural diet options for dogs, discover how to incorporate dietary supplements, and learn about the benefits of a homemade diet.

An increasingly popular option among pet owners is the raw diet, also known as BARF (Biologically Appropriate Raw Food). This diet is based on the idea that dog's benefit from eating food in its most natural, unprocessed form. It consists of providing raw meat, bones, organs and a small number of vegetables and fruits as a supplement. When feeding your dog a raw diet, be sure to do so in a safe and balanced way, consulting a veterinarian or canine nutrition specialist for guidance.

In addition to the raw diet, there are other food supplements that can benefit your dog's health. For example, omega-3 fatty acids, such as those found in krill oil or salmon oil, can help maintain healthy skin and coat, as well as support brain and cardiovascular function. Probiotics, on the other hand, are beneficial microorganisms that promote optimal digestive health. You can find these supplements in the form of oils, powders, or tablets, but it's always important to check with a vet before starting any supplementation.

Another option to consider is home feeding. Preparing your dog's food at home can give you greater control over the ingredients and quality of the food you eat. However, it's essential to ensure that your homemade diet is balanced and provides all the necessary nutrients. Consult a dog nutrition specialist to ensure that you are offering a complete and appropriate diet for your dog.

As with any change in your dog's diet, it's important to make a gradual transition. Introduce new foods slowly and see how your dog tolerates them. Watch for any signs of an upset stomach or changes in behavior, and adjust your diet as needed. Always remember that every dog is unique and may have different dietary needs.

In short, holistic dog food involves understanding that their well-being goes beyond simply providing them with a balanced diet. Consider quality food options, such as a raw diet or home feed, and supplement with food supplements based on your dog's individual needs. Always remember to consult a veterinarian or dog nutrition specialist for appropriate guidance.

In this chapter, we've explored specific guidelines for feeding your dog holistically and ensuring their overall well-being. From choosing quality food to considering natural diet options and dietary supplements, you have the tools you need to take your dog's health to the next level. Enjoy your journey to holistic eating and congratulations on taking steps to improve the life of your beloved pet!

Chapter 6: Holistic Feeding for Cats

L earn how to adapt holistic feeding to cats' unique tastes and needs to keep them happy and healthy.

When it comes to the nutrition of our beloved felines, it's essential to consider their individual tastes and needs. Like us, cats have particular preferences and requirements when it comes to feeding. In this chapter, we'll explore how to adapt holistic feeding to meet the unique demands of our feline companions and ensure their well-being.

Holistic feeding is based on the idea of providing a balanced and natural diet for our cats, taking into account all aspects of their health and happiness. Unlike conventional commercial options, holistic foods are designed to address the physiological and emotional needs of our feline friends.

The first thing we should consider when designing our cats' holistic diet is their overall health status. Each feline is unique and may have special requirements due to allergies, food sensitivities, or a medical condition. Therefore, it is essential to consult with a veterinarian before making significant changes to our pet's diet. The feline health professional will provide us with specific guidance based on our cat's individual needs.

Once we have received approval from our veterinarian, we can begin to adapt our cat's diet to a more holistic approach. This includes focusing on natural, high-quality ingredients, avoiding processed foods full of artificial additives. Opting for food prepared at home or for quality commercial options is an excellent way to ensure that our cat gets the necessary nutrients.

Within the holistic diet for cats, it is essential to meet their protein requirements. Cats are carnivorous animals by nature, so they need an adequate amount of animal protein in their diet. Make sure to offer foods that contain high-quality meat, poultry, or fish, avoiding those that include low-quality animal by-products.

In addition to protein, it is important to consider healthy fats in our cat's diet. Fats provide energy and are vital for the proper development and maintenance of your body. When choosing holistic foods, look for foods that contain healthy fat sources such as salmon, olive oil, or coconut oil. These nutrients will promote healthy skin and coat, as well as the proper functioning of your immune system.

Another key aspect to consider is hydration. Cats tend to drink little water and many suffer from chronic dehydration. To combat this, we can offer foods with a high moisture content, such as cans of wet food or supplement your diet with low-sodium broths. In addition, it is important to provide fresh and clean water in an accessible container so that our cat can stay hydrated throughout the day.

In short, adapting holistic feeding to the unique tastes and needs of our cats is essential to keeping them happy and healthy. Let's remember to consult with a veterinarian to ensure that we are making appropriate dietary choices for our pet. Let's prioritize natural, high-quality ingredients, focusing on healthy proteins and fats, while considering hydration as a key factor in your well-being. Our felines deserve the best, and providing them with a holistic diet is one way to show them our love and care.

End of the first part of chapter 6. When it comes to the holistic nutrition of our beloved felines, it is essential to consider all aspects of their health and well-being. In this second part of chapter 6, we'll explore more practical tips and recommendations to adapt holistic feeding to our cats and keep them happy and healthy.

Another important aspect to consider in holistic feeding for cats is the quantity and frequency of meals. Unlike dogs, cats are naturally hunting animals and consume small portions of food throughout the day. Therefore, it is advisable to offer them several small, frequent meals instead of one or two large meals a day. This will ensure that they are satisfied and will also help prevent problems such as obesity.

If we choose to feed our cats food prepared at home, it's important to ensure that the recipes are balanced and complete in nutrients. Consulting with a veterinarian or feline nutritionist can go a long way in ensuring that we are providing all the essential nutrients in the right amounts. In addition, we can supplement the diet with nutritional supplements such as taurine, an essential amino acid for the eye and heart health of cats.

In the case of choosing holistic commercial food options, we must carefully read the labels and select those brands that use natural, high-quality ingredients. Let's avoid foods that contain low-quality animal by-products, artificial preservatives and dyes. It is advisable to choose options that include recognizable ingredients and that do not contain unnecessary additives.

In addition to food, the environment and the way we present food to our cats can also influence their well-being during meals. Many cats enjoy mental and physical stimulation during mealtime. We can use interactive foods or food dispensing toys to keep them active and mentally stimulated while they eat. This can also help prevent boredom and destructive behavior.

It's important to remember that every cat is unique and may have individual food preferences. Some cats may have food allergies or sensitivities, so we should watch for any signs of discomfort after a meal. If we notice any digestive problems, itchy skin, or other worrisome symptoms, it's critical to see a veterinarian to rule out any underlying health issues.

The second half of this chapter has focused on adapting holistic feeding to the unique tastes and needs of our cats to keep them happy and healthy. By consulting with a veterinarian, prioritizing natural and high-quality ingredients, considering the quantity and frequency of meals, and providing mental stimulation during meals, we will be providing our felines with the best possible nutritional care.

In short, holistic cat food is based on providing a balanced and natural diet that meets all their physical and emotional needs. Let's consider the tips and recommendations presented in this chapter as we adapt the diet of our feline companions. Our cats deserve the best, and providing them with a holistic diet is one way to show them our love and care.

End of chapter 6 on holistic feeding for cats. Keep reading to discover more valuable information about the well-being of our pets.

Chapter 7: Essential Nutritional Supplements

Explore nutritional supplements that can complement your pet's holistic diet and optimize their long-term well-being.

In our quest to ensure a healthy and happy life for our beloved pets, food plays a crucial role. A balanced diet based on natural and quality ingredients is essential for your well-being. However, there are times when the nutrition provided by food is not enough to cover all the needs of our furry companions. This is where nutritional supplements come into play.

Nutritional supplements are products designed to supplement pets' diets and provide them with additional nutrients that may be lacking in their daily diet. These supplements can vary widely, from specific vitamins and minerals to essential fatty acids and probiotics. Its goal is to optimize the health of our pets in the long term, providing them with complete and balanced nutrition.

One of the most common and beneficial supplements for our pets are vitamins. Just like humans, dogs and cats need a variety of essential vitamins for proper bodily function. Vitamins A, B, C, D and E play different roles in our pets' bodies, from strengthening their immune system to contributing to the proper development of their bones and muscles. It's important to note that the amount and type of vitamins your pet needs will depend on several factors, such as their age, breed and health status.

Another key nutritional supplement is essential fatty acids, such as omega-3 and omega-6 fatty acids. These fatty acids play a fundamental role in the health of our pet, as they promote skin and coat health, improve brain function and reduce inflammation. They can be found in sources such as fish oil, linseed oil or coconut oil, among others. Ensuring that your pet receives an adequate amount of essential fatty acids is essential for maintaining a shiny coat and healthy skin, as well as promoting their overall well-being.

The inclusion of probiotics in our pets' diets is also highly beneficial. These living microorganisms promote intestinal health and contribute to a balanced digestive system. Probiotics help improve nutrient absorption, reduce the incidence of digestive disorders and strengthen the immune system of our pets. They can be found in the form of specific supplements or even in fermented foods, such as natural yogurt.

It's important to note that choosing the right nutritional supplements for your pet should be done under the supervision and recommendation of a veterinarian. Every animal is unique and their individual needs may vary. A trusted professional will be able to evaluate your pet's diet, identify possible deficiencies and recommend the most appropriate supplements to improve their health and well-being.

Always remember that nutritional supplements should be considered as a complement to a balanced diet and not as a replacement for quality foods. Providing your pet with a holistic diet, combined with essential nutritional supplements, is a great way to ensure their long-term well-being.

Continued... Essential nutritional supplements play a crucial role in the health and well-being of our pets, but it's important to remember that not every supplement is appropriate or necessary for every pet. Each animal has individual and unique needs that must be evaluated by a trusted veterinarian. In this second half of the chapter, we'll continue to explore some essential nutritional supplements that can benefit your pet.

Another important supplement to consider is glucosamine and chondroitin. These substances help maintain the health of your pet's joints and cartilage, which is especially important for older dogs and cats or those suffering from joint diseases such as arthritis. Glucosamine and chondroitin can reduce inflammation and pain, improve your pet's mobility and quality of life. Consult your veterinarian about the appropriate dosage and method of administration, as glucosamine and chondroitin supplements are often available in different forms.

In addition to the supplements mentioned above, there are others that may be beneficial for some pets in specific situations. For example, if your pet has urinary system problems, such as recurrent infections or kidney stones, cranberry supplements may be helpful. Cranberry contains antibacterial properties that can prevent bacteria from sticking to the urinary tract, reducing the risk of infections. However, it's important to remember that these supplements should be used under the supervision of a veterinarian, as they may interact with other medications or treatments.

In addition, antioxidants are nutritional supplements that can be beneficial for our pets. Antioxidants help neutralize free radicals and protect cells from oxidative damage. This can be especially useful for older pets or those with chronic diseases, as antioxidants can strengthen the immune system and contribute to healthy aging. Some examples of antioxidants used in pet supplements include vitamin E, selenium, and polyphenols.

We cannot forget the importance of maintaining good oral health in our pets. Dental problems are common in dogs and cats, and can affect their overall well-being. Dental supplements can be an additional option to improve your pet's oral health. Some dental supplements are formulated to reduce plaque and tartar formation, while others contain ingredients that promote healthy gums and fresh breath. Remember that these supplements do not replace regular tooth brushing and professional cleanings, but they can be used as a supplement to maintain good oral hygiene.

In conclusion, essential nutritional supplements can be a great way to supplement your pet's holistic diet and optimize their long-term well-being. However, it is essential to always consult with a trusted veterinarian before starting any supplementation. Every pet is unique, and so are their nutritional needs. An animal health professional will be able to evaluate your pet's diet and recommend the most appropriate supplements to improve their health and quality of life. Remember that supplements should be considered as an addition to a balanced diet and not as a replacement for quality foods. Take care of your pet by providing them with a holistic diet and the right essential nutritional supplements for a long and healthy life!

Chapter 8: The Transition to Holistic Eating

Get practical tips to ease the transition from your pet's previous diet to a holistic diet without causing stress.

When we decide to adopt a holistic diet for our pets, it's important to keep in mind that the transition to this new feeding style must be gradual and careful. Our furry friends can be sensitive to sudden changes in their diet, so it's critical to take the right steps to ensure a successful, stress-free transition.

The first step in easing this transition is to research and educate yourself about the benefits of holistic eating. Understanding how natural, unprocessed ingredients can contribute to the overall health and well-being of our pets will help us make informed decisions during this process. In addition, consulting with a veterinarian or an animal nutrition specialist can be of great help, as they can provide us with specific guidelines according to the individual needs and characteristics of our pet.

Once we have acquired the necessary knowledge, it is important to gradually introduce new foods into our pet's diet. Starting with small portions and mixing them with their regular food is an effective strategy to get them used to the taste and texture of new foods. As the transition progresses, we can gradually increase the proportion of holistic food until it becomes the entirety of your diet.

It's essential to keep in mind that every animal is unique and may react differently to changes in its diet. For this reason, it is essential to take a close look at our pet during this transition process. Paying attention to possible signs of digestive distress, such as diarrhea or vomiting, will allow us to identify any problems and make the necessary adjustments in the diet transition.

In addition, it is important to remember that a holistic diet is not only about the food itself, but also about the habits and routine of our pets. Providing a calm and stable environment during the food transition can help reduce stress and facilitate adaptation. Maintaining a regular eating routine and giving them enough time to enjoy their food are essential to encouraging a positive experience during this process.

We must also be prepared to face possible initial resistance or rejection from our pets. Some animals may be cautious or suspicious of changes in their diet, so it may be necessary to use strategies to encourage their interest. Experimenting with different presentations, such as canned or homemade foods, can help them find options that are more appealing to them.

Remember that patience and consistency are key throughout the transition. Each pet has its own pace of adaptation, and it is essential to respect their individual times. If we encounter difficulties or adverse reactions, we can always turn to the guidance of a professional for additional advice.

In short, the transition to a holistic diet can be an enriching process both for our pets and for us as responsible owners. By following these practical tips, we will be providing a positive and healthy experience of change for our beloved pets. Keep your expectations high, because in the next part of this chapter, we will discover how to further enhance the benefits of holistic nutrition and provide our pet with a healthy and happy life. You can't miss it!

(Word count: 733) In the second half of this chapter, we'll continue to explore ways we can maximize the benefits of holistic nutrition for our pets and provide them with healthy, happy lives.

Once we have successfully transitioned to a holistic diet, it's important to remain committed to providing our pets with a balanced and nutritious diet. Variety is key to a holistic diet, as different foods offer different health benefits for our furry friends. We can consider introducing new foods and homemade recipes to add variety to their diet and provide them with a wide range of nutrients.

In addition to food, it is essential to pay attention to other aspects of our pets' lives that can influence their overall health and well-being. Regular exercise is essential to keep our pets in optimal physical and mental condition. Walking, playing and providing them with activity appropriate to their race, size and age will help keep their muscles strong, control their weight and stimulate their minds.

Dental care is also an important aspect of our pets' holistic health. The accumulation of plaque and the development of dental diseases can negatively affect your overall well-being. It is advisable to establish a regular tooth brushing routine, use specific dental products and offer suitable toys that promote teeth cleaning.

In addition, it is essential to keep veterinary visits up to date. Regular checkups make it possible to identify any health problems early and to address them appropriately. In addition, the veterinarian may provide us with specific recommendations on the nutrition and care of our pet, taking into account their individual needs.

Managing stress is also a vital aspect of the well-being of our pets. Chronic stress can negatively affect your physical and mental health. Providing a safe and peaceful environment, giving them enough time to rest, and establishing a daily routine that includes moments of relaxation, can help reduce stress and promote their overall well-being.

Last but not least, emotional connection plays a critical role in our pets' lives. Spending quality time with them, providing them with care and affection, will strengthen the bond we share and provide them with a sense of security and happiness. Communication and mental enrichment are also important to your emotional well-being. Interacting with them through training games, providing them with challenging toys and enriching their environment with stimuli are effective ways to keep our pets mentally active and happy.

In conclusion, holistic feeding is only part of the path to health and happiness for our pets. Supplementing it with regular exercise, dental care, visits to the vet, stress management and a strong emotional connection, will allow us to provide them with a complete and harmonious life. Let us always remember that our pets depend on us for their well-being, so we must strive to provide them with the right care. Our pets deserve it!

Thank you for joining us in this chapter on the transition to a holistic diet. We hope you found these tips useful, and we invite you to continue exploring the path to a healthy and happy life with your beloved pet.

Chapter 9: The Importance of Dietary Balance

Holistic feeding is a philosophy that seeks to provide our pets with a balanced and healthy diet, taking into account all aspects of their well-being. In this chapter, we will delve into the importance of balance in the diet of our beloved pets and how to achieve an adequate balance of nutrients.

Our pets are completely dependent on us for the essential nutrients they need to stay healthy and full of energy. As for us, a balanced diet is essential for the optimal functioning of your body. However, the term "balance" can be somewhat ambiguous, so it's important to understand it in the context of holistic eating.

First of all, you need to understand that every animal is unique and has individual nutritional needs. Some important factors to consider are our pet's age, weight, breed and activity level. These elements give us clues about what type of food and in what proportions should be part of your diet. For example, a growing puppy will need a higher amount of protein and fat for development, while an overweight adult dog will require a lower calorie diet.

However, achieving the right balance of nutrients goes beyond simply meeting the basic needs of our pets. Holistic feeding is based on the idea that animal welfare is interconnected with their food, and therefore, we must consider not only the nutrients we provide to them, but also their quality and origin.

In this regard, it's important to choose high-quality foods that are appropriate for your species. Many commercial foods are full of unhealthy additives, preservatives, and by-products. Opting for a natural and balanced diet means selecting fresh and organic products whenever possible. In addition, we must not forget to include a variety of foods to ensure that we cover all the nutritional needs of our pets.

When it comes to achieving a balance in our pets' holistic diet, it's also crucial to avoid nutrient deficiencies or excesses. A nutritional deficiency can have negative repercussions on your health and well-being. For example, a lack of essential fatty acids can cause skin and coat problems, while a shortage of certain minerals can affect your bone system.

On the other hand, excess nutrients such as vitamins or minerals can be just as harmful. An excess of certain vitamins can cause toxicity in the body of our pets, and an imbalance between certain minerals can interfere with their assimilation and cause long-term problems.

This is why we must take into account both the quality of the food we choose and the quantities in which we provide it. Holistic nutrition seeks an optimal balance of nutrients that ensures the general well-being of our pets, avoiding deficiencies or excesses that could affect their long-term health.

With this brief introduction to the importance of balance in the holistic diet of our pets, we have laid the foundations for understanding its relevance to their well-being and happiness. In the second part of this chapter, we'll explore in greater depth how to achieve the right balance of nutrients through a holistic diet and what specific considerations we need to consider. Don't miss the continuation of this fascinating topic and discover how to ensure the health and happiness of your beloved pet through proper nutrition! In this second part of the chapter, we'll delve into how to achieve the right balance of nutrients through a holistic diet for our pets and the specific considerations we need to consider.

One way to ensure an optimal balance of nutrients is to offer a variety of foods. Just like humans, our pets benefit from a diverse diet that includes different types of proteins, fats, carbohydrates, vitamins and minerals. This provides them with a full range of essential nutrients to maintain optimal health.

When selecting food for our pets, we must pay special attention to the quality of the ingredients. Opting for natural and organic foods can make a big difference in the health and well-being of our furry companions. Avoiding foods that contain unhealthy additives, preservatives and by-products is essential to maintaining a balanced and quality diet.

In addition, it's important to consider the specific needs of each pet. Some breeds may have particular nutritional requirements, and it's important to be informed about these needs. In the same way, the stages of our pet's life can have an impact on their nutritional needs. For example, an older dog may need a lower calorie diet to avoid being overweight and related health problems.

Another key aspect of holistic nutrition is the right proportion of nutrients. Each type of food has a unique composition of proteins, fats and carbohydrates. Finding the right balance between these nutrients is vital to ensuring a balanced diet. For example, some diets may be high in protein but low in fat, while others may have excess carbohydrates. It is important to find the right proportion that fits the individual needs of our pet.

In addition to macronutrients, we must not neglect the importance of micronutrients such as vitamins and minerals. These compounds are essential for the proper functioning of our pets' bodies. However, it's important to remember that an excess of certain vitamins or minerals can be harmful. Therefore, it is critical to follow recommended dosage guidelines and avoid overfeeding supplements.

When choosing a holistic diet for our pets, we must also consider how food is processed and prepared. Processed food tends to lose nutrients during its production, so opting for fresh, quality foods is a good option. By cooking at home for our pets, we can better control the ingredients and ensure that they receive all the necessary nutrients in their diet.

In short, achieving the right balance of nutrients in our pets' holistic diet is critical to their health and well-being. This means offering a variety of quality foods, adjusting nutrient ratios to individual needs, and paying attention to the life stages of our pets. In addition, it is essential to avoid nutrient deficiencies and excesses and to consider the way in which foods are processed and prepared. By following these principles, we can ensure a holistic diet that promotes the health and happiness of our beloved pets.

Chapter 10: Holistic Feeding for Senior Pets

Learn how to adapt holistic feeding to the specific needs of older pets to maintain their vitality and health.

As our beloved pets age, their nutritional needs also change. Like us, the years take their toll on their bodies and it is our responsibility to provide them with adequate nutrition that allows them to stay healthy and full of vitality. In this chapter, we'll dive into the wonderful world of holistic feeding for senior pets.

Holistic feeding is based on the idea that our pets are integral beings, where their physical, emotional and spiritual well-being are closely interrelated. That's why, as with any other stage of life, it's essential to adapt their diet as they age.

When our faithful companions reach old age, they often have specific challenges, such as joint problems, reduced digestive capacity and greater propensity for chronic diseases. Holistic nutrition offers a complete and balanced solution to help them face these challenges and lead full and healthy lives.

The first thing is to consider the quality of the ingredients we use in the diet of our senior pets. Opting for natural, fresh and high-quality foods is essential to provide them with the nutrients they need for their well-being. Avoid products that contain meat by-products, artificial colors or chemical preservatives, as these additives can negatively affect your health.

In addition, it is crucial to adjust food portions to meet the energy needs of a senior pet. As they age, their metabolism slows down and they need fewer calories to maintain a healthy weight. Consult your trusted veterinarian to determine the right amount of food to offer your pet and make regular adjustments based on changes in weight and physical activity.

When it comes to essential nutrients, it's important to make sure your senior pet gets the right amount of protein, fat, vitamins and minerals. High-quality protein is essential for maintaining muscle mass, while healthy fats provide energy and

PROMOTE THE ABSORPTION of fat-soluble vitamins. Don't forget to include a variety of fruits and vegetables in your diet for natural vitamins and antioxidants.

Another key aspect of holistic nutrition for senior pets is caring for their digestive system. Over the years, it's common for them to experience decreased production of digestive enzymes, which can lead to food intolerances and digestive discomfort. To counter this, consider including probiotics and digestive enzymes in your diet. These supplements will help maintain a healthy intestinal balance and improve nutrient absorption.

In short, adapting holistic feeding to the specific needs of senior pets is essential to ensure a healthy and happy life at this stage of their lives. Providing them with high-quality food, adjusting portions and taking care of their digestive system are some of the key aspects to consider. Always remember to consult with a veterinary professional for personalized guidance and to ensure that you are providing them with the best dietary care.

Don't miss the second part of this chapter, where we'll discover how to incorporate stimulating exercises and activities to keep our senior pets at their best! In addition to proper nutrition, there are other important aspects that we must consider to keep our senior pets in their best shape. In this second part of the chapter, we'll discover how to incorporate stimulating exercises and activities to ensure your physical and mental well-being.

Regular exercise is key to keeping our senior pets active and in good shape. While it is important to adapt the intensity and duration of the exercises to their specific needs, we must not forget that they still need physical activity to maintain a healthy weight and strengthen their muscle mass.

A great option is to take regular walks, but it's important to adjust the intensity and duration taking into account your physical condition. Gentle, leisurely walks can be beneficial for maintaining mobility and cardiovascular health. It's important to pay attention to the signs that tell us if they're tired or uncomfortable during the ride, and adjust accordingly.

In addition to walking, we can incorporate softer activities such as stretching exercises or swimming to help maintain flexibility and prevent joint stiffness. It's also important to provide them with interactive toys that stimulate their mind and help them stay mentally agile.

Mental stimulation is essential for our senior pets. We can do this through search games, where we hide treats or toys and allow them to find them. There are also puzzles and intelligence games designed especially for pets, providing them with a cognitive challenge and entertainment.

Another activity that can be very beneficial for our senior pets is animal-assisted therapy. This therapy involves interacting with other animals, such as dogs or cats, that are specially trained to provide companionship and emotional support. These interactions can promote relaxation, emotional and social well-being for our pets.

It's important to remember that, as with any physical activity, we must consider the individual limitations and needs of our senior pets. Always consult your veterinarian before starting any new exercise program and be sure to adapt it to your pet's specific needs.

In addition to a balanced diet and exercise, it is also important to pay attention to other aspects of the care and well-being of our senior pets. Maintaining a comfortable and safe environment is essential to your health and peace of mind.

It's important to make sure they have a comfortable place to rest and sleep. Orthopedic beds can be especially beneficial in relieving pressure on joints and providing adequate support.

In addition, we must pay attention to the hygiene and personal care of our senior pets. This includes regularly brushing their fur to remove dead hair and prevent tangling, as well as keeping their nails short and clean.

Finally, let's not forget to provide them with lots of love and attention. Spending quality time with our senior pets strengthens our bond with them and provides them with a sense of security and emotional well-being.

In conclusion, adapting holistic nutrition to the specific needs of our senior pets is just one part of the comprehensive care we must offer them. Ensuring that we provide them with adequate exercise, stimulating activities and a comfortable and safe environment will allow us to keep our senior pets healthy, happy and full of vitality at this stage of their lives.

Always remember to consult with a veterinary professional for personalized guidance and be sure to provide them with the best care in all areas of their lives. Taking these recommendations into account, you can enjoy many more years with your faithful companion!

Chapter 11: The Relationship Between Eating and Behavior

Explore how a holistic diet can influence your pet's behavior and help address problems such as anxiety or hyperactivity.

In the world of pets, behavior plays a crucial role in how they interact with us and their environment. Sometimes, however, we can encounter behavioral problems in our beloved pets, such as anxiety, hyperactivity or even aggressiveness. These behaviors can affect both the quality of life of our pets and our own relationship with them. Fortunately, the answer to these difficulties may be closer than we think: on your plate of food.

Holistic feeding has become an increasingly popular option among pet owners looking for better health and well-being for their furry companions. But what exactly is holistic eating? Unlike traditional food, which focuses mainly on alleviating hunger and meeting basic nutrient needs, holistic feeding considers the pet as a whole, taking into account not only their physique but also their mind and spirit.

When we talk about holistic feeding, we refer to the choice of natural foods, without artificial additives or processed ingredients, that are beneficial to the overall health and well-being of our pet. This involves looking for high-quality, nutritionally balanced foods that provide the nutrients necessary to maintain an optimal state of health and vitality.

The relationship between food and the behavior of our pets should not be underestimated. Just like humans, what they eat can have a direct impact on their mood, energy level, ability to concentrate, and even their ability to manage stress. A poor diet can lead to nutritional imbalances that negatively affect our pet's behavior.

Anxiety is one of the most common behavioral problems in dogs and cats. If your pet shows signs of nervousness, restlessness, or excessive fear, their diet may be affecting their emotional state. Some studies suggest that certain ingredients in commercial food may increase sensitivity to stress in pets, resulting in a greater propensity for anxiety.

In addition to anxiety, hyperactivity can also be related to eating. An excess of rapidly absorbed carbohydrates, present in some processed foods, can cause a sudden increase in energy in our pet, leading them to behave impulsively and unrestrained. On the other hand, a balanced diet, rich in essential nutrients such as omega-3 fatty acids, B vitamins and minerals, can help promote calm and emotional stability.

Holistic eating can become a powerful tool for addressing these behavioral issues. By offering our pets natural and nutritious food, we provide them with the necessary elements to maintain physical and mental balance. In the second half of this chapter, we will delve into how we can implement holistic nutrition in the daily lives of our pets and what aspects we must consider when choosing the right foods.

Remember, our pets also deserve a healthy and happy life. By understanding the close relationship between diet and behavior, we can make a difference in the quality of life of our precious companions. Keep reading to discover more about the powerful connection between holistic nutrition and balanced, harmonious behavior in our pets! In the second half of this chapter, we will explore how to implement holistic nutrition in the daily lives of our pets and what aspects we should consider when choosing the right foods.

When we talk about holistic nutrition, in addition to selecting natural and nutritious foods, we must also consider the quality of the ingredients used. It's important to pay attention to where the meat, chicken, or fish used in pet food comes from. Choosing foods that use high-quality, sustainably sourced proteins is essential to ensure adequate nutrition.

Another aspect to consider is to avoid foods that contain artificial additives, dyes or chemical preservatives. These ingredients can have a negative impact on the health of our pets and, in some cases, can even increase behavioral problems. Opting for food free of artificial ingredients is one way to ensure that we are providing our pets with a natural and healthy diet.

Choosing a holistic diet also involves considering the individual needs of our pet. Every pet is unique and has specific nutritional requirements, which can be influenced by their breed, age, size and activity level. Before making changes to our pet's diet, it's important to check with a veterinarian to make sure we're providing the necessary nutrients in the right amounts.

In addition to selecting the right foods, we must also pay attention to how we feed our pets. Establishing regular feeding times and avoiding overfeeding can contribute to a more balanced behavior. Many times, the way we feed our pets can reinforce certain unwanted behaviors. For example, if we feed our pet every time they demand food, we may be reinforcing anxiety or hyperactivity. Establishing routines and limiting food rewards to appropriate times can help establish healthy habits and promote a balanced relationship with food.

In addition to food, it is also important to consider other aspects of our pets' lives that may influence their behavior. Regular exercise, environmental enrichment and adequate socialization also play a crucial role in the emotional well-being of our pets. A holistic diet combined with these other cares gives us a comprehensive perspective to promote healthy and happy behavior in our pets.

In short, holistic feeding offers a powerful tool to improve the behavior of our pets. By providing them with natural and nutritious food, we are providing them with the elements necessary to maintain physical and mental balance. By choosing high-quality food, avoiding artificial additives, and considering each pet's individual needs, we're helping to address issues such as anxiety and hyperactivity.

A holistic diet combined with other appropriate care, such as exercise and socialization, allows us to provide our pets with a healthy and happy life. In addition, it gives us the opportunity to strengthen and improve our relationship with them.

As pet owners, our responsibility is to provide them with the best possible care. By understanding the close relationship between diet and behavior, we can make a difference in the quality of life of our precious companions. Let's continue to explore the powerful connection between holistic nutrition and balanced and harmonious behavior in our pets!

Chapter 12: Homemade Recipes for Holistic Eating

Discover delicious homemade recipes that you can prepare for your pet and provide them with a holistic diet made with love.

In this chapter, we want to share with you some homemade recipes that are sure to make your pet feel loved and loved. Holistic feeding is about offering our pets a balanced diet using natural and fresh ingredients. In addition, preparing food at home allows us to have greater control over what our animals consume and gives us the possibility to seek alternatives for those pets with special needs or food sensitivities.

It is always important to remember that before making any changes to our pet's diet, especially if they have a medical condition or are following a specific diet for veterinary advice, it is essential to consult an animal health professional. This will ensure that our actions are the right ones and that we are providing our pets with the best possible food.

As for homemade recipes, here we will share some ideas for you to get down to work in the kitchen and pamper your faithful companion. Each recipe is designed with our pets' nutrition in mind, but also their enjoyment and happiness.

We'll start with a recipe for cats, as we know how selective they can be when it comes to eating. This recipe for "Chicken and Pumpkin Pate" is a healthy and flavorful option that will surely conquer your kitty's palate. You'll need:

- 1 cooked and shredded chicken breast
- 1/4 cup of pumpkin puree
- 1 tablespoon of olive oil

- 1 beaten egg.
- 2 tablespoons of brown rice flour

In a bowl, mix the shredded chicken with the pumpkin puree and olive oil. Then, add the beaten egg and brown rice flour. Mix all the ingredients until you get a homogeneous mass. Once the dough is ready, you can form small balls and crush them slightly to obtain the desired "pâté" shape. Then, place the balls on a baking sheet and cook them in the preheated oven at 180°C for approximately 15 minutes or until golden brown.

This recipe is ideal for pampering your cat with a healthy, protein-packed snack. In addition, pumpkin will provide you with fiber and help maintain a healthy digestive system.

Now, for dog lovers, we have a delicious and nutritious option. The recipe for "Oatmeal and Apple Cookies" will be the perfect gift to reward your loyal friend. You'll need:
- 1 cup of whole wheat flour
- 1 cup of oatmeal
- 1 grated apple.
- 1 egg.
- 1/4 cup of melted coconut oil

In a bowl, mix the whole wheat flour and oatmeal. Then, add the grated apple, egg, and melted coconut oil. Knead all the ingredients well until you get a smooth and homogeneous dough. Then, roll out the dough with a rolling pin and use cookie cutters to shape your canine cookies.

Place the cookies on a baking sheet and cook them in the preheated oven at 180°C for approximately 20 minutes or until golden brown.

These homemade cookies are an excellent option to reward your dog during training or simply to pamper him at any time of the day. The oats will provide fiber and energy, while the apple will provide antioxidants and an irresistible flavor.

These are just two of the many homemade recipes you can prepare for your pet! In the second part of this chapter, we'll surprise you with more nutritious and delicious options to continue nourishing your life partner holistically.

Don't miss the sequel in the next installment, where you'll find recipes for rodents, birds and reptiles. The culinary adventure to pamper your pet is about to continue! Welcome back! In the second part of this chapter on homemade recipes for holistic eating, we'll continue to explore nutritious and delicious options to pamper your pet. There's nothing better than preparing home-cooked meals using natural, fresh ingredients to give your furry companion the love and attention they deserve. Let's keep cooking!

We continue with a recipe for rodents, specifically for those adorable guinea pigs. These small creatures are very sensitive to their food, so it is essential to provide them with a diet rich in fiber and nutrients. The recipe for "Assorted Vegetable Salad" is a perfect option to meet your nutritional needs. You'll need:

- 1 grated carrot.
- 1 fresh pea.
- 1 spinach leaf.
- 1 slice of cucumber.
- 1 slice of red pepper

On a plate, place all the vegetables and mix them gently. Make sure to cut them into small pieces that are easy for your guinea pig to chew. Fresh vegetables will provide fiber and vitamins essential to your health. Remember that it is important to wash vegetables thoroughly before serving them, eliminating any residue or pesticides. Your guinea pig will thank you!

For those who own birds, their feathered friends will love this recipe. The recipe for "Seed Energy Balls" is an ideal option to provide them with a tasty and healthy snack. You'll need:

- 1/4 cup of sunflower seeds

- 1/4 cup of pumpkin seeds
- 1/4 cup of chia seeds
- 1/4 cup of honey.

In a bowl, mix all the seeds together with the honey and mix until you get a sticky mass. Then, form small balls and let them air dry for a few hours. These energy balls are an excellent source of healthy protein and fatty acids for your birds. You'll see how they enjoy them!

Last but not least, we have an option to pamper those fabulous cold-blooded pets: reptiles. Although their nutritional needs are different, it's always important to provide them with a balanced, species-appropriate diet. The recipe for "Fruit and Vegetable Shake" is perfect to offer them a fresh food full of vitamins. You'll need:

- 1 spinach leaf.
- 1 slice of cucumber.
- 1/4 of an apple.
- 1/4 carrot.
- 1/4 cup of water.

In a blender, mix all the ingredients until you get a smooth consistency. Serve the shake on a platter and watch your reptile feast on this refreshing and nourishing food. Remember to research the specific needs of your particular reptile and adjust the recipe as needed.

Congratulations! You've learned some delicious homemade recipes to pamper your pet and provide them with a holistic diet. Remember that these are just a few options and that you can experiment with different ingredients and combinations to adapt them to the needs and preferences of your furry companion.

We hope you enjoyed this chapter and are inspired to prepare healthy and delicious meals for your pets. Always remember to check with an animal health professional before making any changes to your pet's diet, especially if they have a medical condition or are following a specific diet.

See you in the next chapter, where we'll explore more tips and recipes to keep our pets happy and healthy. See you soon!

Chapter 13: Holistic Eating Versus Processed Foods

Feeding our pets is a fundamental part of their overall well-being and happiness. Over the years, we have witnessed how a balanced and healthy diet can make a big difference in the quality of life of our beloved colleagues. That's why in this chapter we're going to explore the benefits of a holistic diet compared to the risks and drawbacks of processed foods.

Holistic feeding is based on a comprehensive approach to nourishing our pets. This involves taking into account not only the quality of the ingredients used, but also the way they are processed and how they affect the overall health of our faithful four-legged friends.

One of the main benefits of opting for a holistic diet is the quality of the ingredients used. Holistic foods are usually composed of natural and fresh ingredients, avoiding the use of artificial additives, preservatives and low-quality by-products. This ensures that our pets are getting the nutrients they need to stay healthy and energetic.

In addition, holistic foods are often easier for our pets to digest. By avoiding artificial additives and ingredients, we reduce the risk of developing food sensitivities and digestive problems. Many pet owners have noticed an improvement in the gastrointestinal well-being of their companions by switching to a holistic diet.

Another important aspect to consider is the amount of processing that food undergoes before it reaches our pets' plates. Processed foods, such as commercial croquettes, often go through an intense industrial process that can affect the quality and nutrients present in them. In addition, the high temperatures used during processing can damage some essential vitamins and minerals.

In contrast, holistic foods are characterized by being less processed and preserving much of their natural nutrients. This translates into greater bioavailability of vitamins and minerals, allowing our pets to take full advantage of the benefits of a balanced diet.

However, it's important to recognize that processed foods also have their place in our pets' diets. The convenience and availability of commercial kibble can sometimes be a determining factor for busy pet owners. In addition, some processed foods are specifically formulated to address special dietary needs, such as allergies or chronic diseases.

In short, holistic feeding offers numerous benefits for the health and well-being of our pets. Natural ingredients, digestibility and less processing are key aspects to consider when making informed food decisions for our faithful companions. However, we should not completely rule out processed foods, as under certain circumstances they can be a valid and convenient option.

It will continue in the second part of the chapter...

A fundamental aspect to consider when choosing between a holistic diet and processed foods is the impact on the long-term health of our pets. Although processed foods can be convenient and apparently easy to offer, it's essential to consider the associated risks and disadvantages.

One of the common concerns with processed foods is the content of artificial additives and preservatives. These additional ingredients can have negative effects on our pets' long-term health. Some studies have linked the consumption of these additives to health problems, such as allergies, immune system diseases and digestive disorders.

On the other hand, holistic foods are usually free of artificial additives and preservatives. Choosing a holistic diet can help reduce the risk of our pets developing food sensitivities and allergies. In addition, by avoiding artificial ingredients, we are providing our pets with a more natural and balanced diet, which can contribute to better long-term health and well-being.

Another factor to consider is the quality of the ingredients used in processed foods compared to holistic foods. Processed foods often contain low-quality by-products and ingredients that are not beneficial to the health of our pets. These by-products can include animal parts that are unfit for human consumption, such as feathers or claws.

In contrast, holistic foods are often made up of natural, fresh ingredients. By choosing a holistic diet, we are providing our pets with high-quality ingredients that are suitable for consumption and that contain the nutrients necessary for their well-being. This can contribute to greater vitality, energy and overall health for our pets.

In addition, the way processed foods are processed can affect the amount of nutrients available to our pets. During processing, essential vitamins and minerals can be lost or damaged due to the high temperatures used. This can result in a less balanced diet for our pets and a lower absorption of important nutrients.

On the contrary, holistic foods are characterized by being less processed and, therefore, preserving a greater amount of natural nutrients. This allows for greater bioavailability of vitamins and minerals, meaning that our pets can take full advantage of the benefits of a balanced diet.

In conclusion, when comparing holistic eating to processed foods, it's important to consider the benefits and risks associated with each option. While processed foods can be convenient, holistic eating provides high-quality ingredients and less processing, which can contribute to better long-term health and well-being for our pets.

As responsible pet owners, we must make informed decisions about feeding our pets, considering their individual needs and consulting with animal nutrition professionals. By choosing a holistic diet, we are investing in the health and happiness of our pets, providing them with the right nutrients and food balance for a full and healthy life.

Chapter 14: How to Read Pet Food Labels

Learn to interpret food labels to ensure that you are choosing quality and suitable products for your pet.

When it comes to feeding our beloved pets, it's essential to understand how to read and understand the labels of the food we buy. After all, we want to ensure that our faithful companions have a balanced and nutritious diet that keeps them healthy and happy. However, with the wealth of information and technical terms found on these labels, it can be overwhelming to know what is most important and what we should avoid.

First and foremost, we must pay attention to the list of ingredients. This is located on the back or side of the container and shows the main components of the pet food. The ingredients are presented in descending order, which means that the first are the ones that are found in greater quantity. It's essential to look for foods that have a quality animal protein source, such as meat, chicken or fish, listed as the first ingredient. This ensures that your pet receives the nutrients it needs to maintain its health and vitality.

Another important aspect to consider is the presence of additives and preservatives. Some pet foods include artificial substances that can be harmful to your long-term health. When reading the label, avoid those that contain high levels of dyes, artificial flavors and meat by-products. Choose foods that use natural preservatives such as vitamin E or rosemary. Remember, choosing a natural and healthy diet will contribute to your pet's well-being.

In addition to the ingredients, it's essential to understand the nutritional information on the labels. This is where we will find the protein, fat and carbohydrate content, as well as the vitamins and minerals that the food provides to our pet. It is important to consider the specific needs of our pet according to their age, size and activity level. For example, puppies require foods with a higher protein content to promote optimal growth, while adult dogs may benefit from a low-fat diet to maintain a healthy weight. Don't forget to check with your vet to ensure that you're providing your pet with adequate nutrition.

Nutritional information also gives us an insight into the caloric intake of food. If your pet has a tendency to gain weight, it's essential to review the calories per recommended serving and adjust the amounts accordingly. Also, keep in mind that the quality of the ingredients influences the digestibility of the food. By choosing high-quality foods, you'll be ensuring that your pet gets the most out of nutrients and efficiently absorbs the elements essential to their well-being.

In short, when reading pet food labels, we must pay attention to the list of ingredients, avoiding those that are artificial or of low quality. In addition, we must consider the specific nutritional needs of our pet and ensure that the food is appropriate for their age and size. Remember that choosing a holistic and quality diet will make a difference in the health and happiness of your faithful companion.

Now that you understand the importance of reading pet food labels and how to interpret nutritional information and key ingredients, it's time to dive into other things to consider when choosing the right food for your pet.

One of these aspects is the presence of allergens in pet food. Like humans, some pets may have allergies or sensitivities to certain ingredients. It's essential to check the list of ingredients for any substance that could cause an allergic reaction in your pet. Common allergens in pet food include wheat, corn, soy, and dairy. If your pet shows signs of allergy such as itching, redness, or digestive problems, you may need to opt for hypoallergenic foods or eliminate allergens from their diet.

Another important consideration is the type of diet you want to provide for your pet. There are several options available, such as dry, canned, raw, or homemade foods. Each type of food has its own advantages and disadvantages, so it's important to find the right balance for your pet. Dry foods are convenient and usually cheaper, but make sure they contain the nutrients you need for a balanced diet. Canned foods may be more appealing to demanding palates and contain a greater amount of water, which can be beneficial for keeping your pet hydrated. Raw, homemade foods provide a natural, fresh diet, but they require more time and effort to prepare them properly.

In addition to considering the type of diet, you must also consider your pet's specific needs in terms of age, size, and health condition. Young and growing pets need more calories and nutrients to promote optimal development, while older pets may require a low-fat diet to control weight and reduce the burden on their joints. If your pet has a specific health condition, such as allergies, digestive problems, or tooth sensitivity, you may need to look for foods that are specially formulated to address these concerns.

Last but not least, remember that your vet is your best ally when it comes to making nutritional decisions for your pet. They know your pet's specific needs and can provide you with personalized recommendations based on their medical history and current health status. Don't hesitate to ask them if you have any questions or concerns about feeding your pet.

In conclusion, reading and understanding pet food labels is essential to ensure an adequate and healthy diet for your pet. By paying attention to the list of ingredients, the presence of additives and preservatives, nutritional information and other aspects such as allergens and type of diet, you will be making informed and responsible decisions for the benefit of your pet's health and happiness.

Remember that choosing a holistic and quality diet is the secret to having a healthy and happy pet. Continue to learn about holistic feeding in the following chapters, where we'll explore topics such as the importance of hydration, the benefits of nutritional supplements, and how to create a balanced homemade diet for your pet.

Your faithful companion deserves the best, so continue to provide them with conscious and nutritious food so they can enjoy a long and vibrant life!

Chapter 15: Holistic Feeding for Pets with Medical Conditions

Learn how to adapt holistic feeding to address your pet's specific medical conditions and promote their well-being.

When we become pet owners, we take responsibility for providing them with love, care and adequate nutrition for their health and happiness. However, some pets may have medical conditions that require special attention to their diet. In this chapter, we'll explore how holistic feeding can help our beloved pets cope with various medical conditions and maintain their overall well-being.

Holistic feeding is based on the principle that all aspects of a pet's life are interconnected and related to their health. This approach considers both the physical and emotional aspects of our pets. By choosing a holistic diet, we are opting for a balanced, quality diet that promotes overall health and well-being.

When it comes to pets with medical conditions, it's essential to adapt their diet according to their specific needs. Some common conditions in pets include food allergies, digestive problems, heart disease, obesity, and kidney disease, among others. Next, we'll explore some recommendations for addressing these medical conditions through holistic eating.

For pets with food allergies, it's important to identify foods that cause them allergic reactions and eliminate them from their diet. Holistic nutrition is based on natural, quality ingredients, making it easier to find options free of common allergens, such as wheat, corn or soy. Opting for hypoallergenic and nutritious foods can help relieve allergy symptoms and promote better health for your pet.

When our pets experience digestive problems, holistic feeding can help restore balance to their digestive system. Opting for foods rich in fiber and probiotics can promote better digestion and combat problems such as diarrhea or constipation. In addition, it's important to offer foods that are easy to digest and avoid those that contain artificial ingredients or chemical additives.

In the case of heart disease, holistic feeding can play a vital role in managing your pet's condition. Choosing foods that are low in sodium and saturated fat can help maintain a healthy heart. In addition, including ingredients rich in omega-3 fatty acids, such as salmon or fish oil, can support heart health and reduce the risk of complications.

Obesity is a common problem in pets and can have a significant impact on their overall health. Holistic eating emphasizes balance and moderation, avoiding excess processed foods and saturated fat. Controlling portions and choosing foods that are low in calories, but rich in nutrients are essential to tackling obesity. In addition, regular exercise and play are also critical to maintaining a healthy weight.

In cases of kidney disease, holistic nutrition can be of great help to the well-being of our pets. Choosing foods low in protein and phosphorus, but rich in essential vitamins and minerals, can support kidney health and reduce the burden on the kidneys. In addition, it is important to keep our pets hydrated, offering them fresh and clean water at all times.

Holistic feeding offers a comprehensive approach to addressing medical conditions specific to our pets. Adapting your diet to your individual needs can make a big difference to your overall health and well-being. In the second part of this chapter, we'll explore more medical conditions and how holistic eating can play a critical role in addressing them. Keep reading to discover more valuable tips and secrets to keeping your pet healthy and happy!

In the second part of this chapter, we will continue to explore other common medical conditions in pets and how holistic feeding can be beneficial to their management and well-being.

For pets with joint problems, such as arthritis, holistic feeding can play an important role in alleviating their symptoms and promoting mobility. Opting for foods rich in omega-3 fatty acids, such as fish oil or krill oil, can help reduce joint inflammation and relieve pain. In addition, there are natural supplements, such as glucosamine and chondroitin, that can be beneficial to your pet's joint health.

For pets with skin problems, such as dermatitis or skin allergies, holistic feeding can help improve the health of their skin and coat. Opting for foods rich in omega-6 fatty acids and zinc can promote healthy skin and reduce itching and irritation. In addition, eliminating artificial ingredients and chemical additives from your diet can decrease the likelihood of allergic reactions.

Some pets may also face medical conditions related to aging, such as decreased cognitive function or loss of mobility. Holistic eating can be of great help in managing these conditions. Opting for foods enriched with antioxidants, such as fruits and vegetables, can promote brain health and reduce cognitive decline. In addition, in this case, it is important to adapt your pet's diet according to their activity level to avoid weight gain and maintain their mobility.

Another common medical condition in pets is diabetes. Holistic eating can play a critical role in managing this disease. Opting for low-carb, high-fiber foods can help regulate your pet's blood glucose levels. In addition, it is important to establish regular eating schedules and to control portions to avoid fluctuations in blood sugar levels.

Last but not least, some pets can experience dental problems, such as plaque build-up and periodontal disease. Holistic nutrition can help maintain good dental health in your pet. Opting for quality, fiber-rich dry foods can promote dental hygiene and reduce plaque build-up. In addition, there are foods specifically designed to help clean teeth, such as textured croquettes or dental toys.

In conclusion, holistic feeding can be a powerful tool for addressing a wide variety of medical conditions in our pets. Adapting your diet according to your individual needs can make a big difference in your overall health and well-being. Remember that every pet is unique and it's important to work with a veterinarian to create an appropriate feeding plan. Holistic feeding, combined with love and care, can promote the health and happiness of your beloved pets.

I hope this information has been useful to you and that you can apply it to your pet's diet. In the next chapter, we'll explore how holistic feeding can promote the mental and emotional health of our pets. Don't miss it! Keep reading to discover more valuable tips and secrets to keep your pet healthy and happy!

Chapter 16: The Dangers of Additives and Preservatives

Discover the risks associated with the additives and preservatives found in processed foods and how to avoid them in a holistic diet.

In the search for a healthy and balanced diet for our faithful furry companions, it is essential to understand the risks that certain additives and preservatives present in processed foods can pose to their health. Although it is common to find these substances in commercial pet food, we must be aware of the dangers they entail and explore more natural alternatives.

Additives, as the name suggests, are substances added to foods with the purpose of improving their appearance, flavor, texture or extending their shelf life. However, some of these additives are potentially harmful to the health of our pets. For example, propylene glycol, a common preservative in pet food, has shown negative effects on the gastrointestinal and renal systems of animals. Similarly, the artificial dye known as tartrazine has been linked to allergic reactions and digestive problems in dogs and cats.

In addition to the best-known additives, there are preservatives used in pet food that can also pose risks to your health. One of them is BHA (butylhydroxyanisole), a synthetic antioxidant used to prevent the rancidity of fats in foods. Studies have shown that BHA can have negative effects on the liver and kidney of animals, and has been associated with the development of cancer in some cases. It's also important to mention sodium nitrite, another common preservative in pet food, which has been linked to health problems such as anemia and damage to the circulatory system.

Holistic feeding seeks to avoid the consumption of these harmful additives and preservatives, providing our pets with a nutritious option free of harmful chemical components. Opting for natural and fresh food is one of the best decisions we can make for the well-being of our furry companions.

In the next chapter, we'll explore the impact of additives and preservatives on the health of our pets and how we can replace them with healthier options in our holistic diet. We'll discover a variety of natural ingredients and strategies to ensure that our faithful companions enjoy balanced, risk-free nutrition.

Keep reading and be surprised by the alternatives we have for you in the second part of this fascinating chapter. You won't be able to resist caring for and feeding your pet in a healthy and happy way. We look forward to seeing you in the next installment! In this second half of the chapter, we will continue to explore the risks associated with the additives and preservatives present in processed pet foods and how we can replace them with healthier options in our holistic diet.

One of the most common preservatives in pet food is BHT (butylhydroxytoluene), which is used to protect food from oxidation and spoilage. However, several studies have linked this preservative to adverse effects on animal health. BHT has been associated with liver and kidney problems, as well as with the development of cancer in some cases.

In addition to BHT, it is also important to mention other preservatives such as calcium propionate, which is used to prevent the growth of mold and mildew in pet food. However, this preservative has been linked to gastrointestinal problems and allergies in some animals.

To avoid these risks, it's critical to read pet food labels carefully and choose options that don't contain harmful additives or preservatives.

Opting for natural and fresh food is an excellent alternative to ensure the health and well-being of our pets.

In addition, we can incorporate foods rich in natural antioxidants into our pets' diets to help protect their antioxidant systems. These foods include fruits and vegetables such as carrots, apples and blueberries, which are excellent sources of essential vitamins and minerals.

It is also important to remember that holistic feeding is not only about avoiding harmful additives and preservatives, but also about providing a balanced and complete diet for our pets. This means including a variety of foods that cover all the nutritional needs of our furry companions.

Instead of relying solely on processed foods, we can include options such as fresh meat, fish and eggs in our pets' diets. These foods are rich in protein and healthy fats, which are essential components for a balanced diet.

In addition, we can consider the option of preparing our pets' meals ourselves. This gives us greater control over the ingredients and ensures that we are providing a high-quality diet without harmful additives or preservatives.

However, it is important to consult a veterinarian before making any changes to our pet's diet. The vet will be able to provide us with specific recommendations and ensure that we are providing all the nutrients necessary for our pet's health.

In short, the additives and preservatives in processed pet foods can pose risks to your health. Holistic nutrition, based on natural and fresh foods, offers us healthier and safer alternatives. By carefully choosing the foods we offer to our pets, we can ensure a long and healthy life for our faithful furry companions.

I hope this second part of the chapter has provided valuable information about the dangers of additives and preservatives, as well as about healthier options in holistic eating. Keep reading to discover more tips and strategies in the coming chapters. Your pet deserves the best!

Chapter 17: The Importance of Hydration in Holistic Eating

Learn why adequate hydration is essential in holistic feeding and how to ensure that your pet is getting enough water.

Hydration is an essential aspect of the life of any living being, including our beloved pets. Just like us, animals need to maintain an optimal level of hydration to enjoy good health and vitality. In this chapter, we'll explore the importance of hydration in holistic eating and provide you with practical tips to ensure your furry companion gets the right amount of water.

First, it's important to understand why hydration is crucial in holistic eating. Holistic feeding is based on providing our pets with a balanced and nutritionally complete diet, taking into account all aspects of their well-being. Adequate nutrition plays a critical role in preventing diseases and promoting healthy living. And within that nutrition, hydration occupies a central place.

Water is vital for the proper functioning of all systems in our pet's body. It helps digest food, regulates body temperature, lubricates joints and plays a crucial role in transporting nutrients and eliminating toxins. Without adequate hydration, our precious furry friends can experience various health issues, such as electrolyte imbalances, dehydration, and even kidney problems.

Now, how can you ensure that your pet is getting enough water? Here are some tips to help you create a healthy hydration habit for your furry companion:

1. Provide fresh, clean water: Make sure your pet always has access to fresh, clean water. Change the water regularly to avoid the accumulation of bacteria and other contaminants that can affect your pet's health.

2. It offers multiple water sources: Place water containers in different places in the house so that your pet always finds water available, whether in the rest area, kitchen or garden. This will make it easier for your pet to hydrate on a regular basis.

3. Consider your pet's preferences: Some pets may prefer to drink water from a larger or shaped container. Observe your partner's preferences and adapt to provide the best hydration experience.

4. Consider using special water fountains: There are water fountains specially designed for pets, which simulate moving water flows and may be more attractive to pets. These fountains can promote hydration and make drinking water a more pleasant experience.

Remember that every pet is unique, so it's important to pay attention to their individual needs. Some breeds or sizes may require larger amounts of water, especially during hot weather or if they engage in intense physical activity. Talk to your vet for personalized recommendations on how much water your pet should consume daily.

In a partial conclusion, adequate hydration is a fundamental pillar in the holistic diet of our pets. Providing them with fresh and clean water, creating regular drinking habits and being aware of the individual needs of each animal are key actions to ensure that they receive the necessary hydration. In the second part of this chapter, we'll delve deeper into the impact of hydration on the health of our pets and explore additional strategies to ensure their well-being. Don't miss it! 5. Get creative: If your pet doesn't show much interest in drinking water, you can try being creative to encourage them to hydrate. For example, you can add some low-sodium chicken broth to the water to give it a different, more appealing flavor. You can also try freezing some pieces of fruit such as strawberries or watermelon and adding them to the water as a refreshing treat. Surely your furry companion will be delighted with these options!

6. Keep the water dishes clean: As with the food bowl, it's important to regularly wash your pet's water dishes. This will prevent bacteria from accumulating and ensure that they always have access to fresh, clean water. Use mild detergent and rinse properly to remove any residue.

7. Watch for signs of dehydration: Even if you're applying all of these recommendations, it's essential that you watch out for possible signs of dehydration in your pet. Some of the indicators may include lethargy, lack of appetite, dry gums or skin, and a decrease in urine production. If you notice any of these symptoms, be sure to contact your veterinarian immediately.

8. Consider alternatives to dry food: If your pet is struggling to get enough hydration through water, you can consider incorporating wet food into their diet. Whether by including canned food or preparing homemade food, these products usually contain a higher proportion of water than dry food, which can help keep your pet hydrated.

Remember that every pet is unique and may have different hydration needs. In addition, climate, activity level and age can also influence how much water your pet needs. It's always a good idea to check with your vet for personalized recommendations for your furry companion.

In short, adequate hydration is a crucial aspect in the holistic nutrition of our pets. By implementing healthy habits, such as providing fresh, clean water, creating multiple water sources, considering your pet's preferences, and being creative, you can ensure that your furry friend gets the right amount of fluid to maintain their health and well-being.

In addition, it's important to be alert to signs of dehydration and consider alternatives to dry food if your pet is having trouble hydrating properly. Remember that your veterinarian is your best ally to obtain specific information and recommendations for the care and nutrition of your pet.

In the next chapter, we'll further explore the impact of hydration on our pets' health and address additional tips to ensure they receive the necessary hydration. Don't miss it! Your pet will thank you.

Chapter 18: Holistic nutrition in times of allergies and sensitivities

Learn how holistic feeding can help alleviate allergies and food sensitivities in your pet, improving their quality of life.

In recent decades, allergies and food sensitivities in pets have been on the rise. This phenomenon has led pet owners to seek effective solutions to alleviate symptoms and improve the health of their beloved furry companions. It is in this context that holistic eating has emerged as a promising and natural option to address these conditions.

Holistic feeding is based on the idea of treating pets in a comprehensive way, taking into account their physical, emotional and spiritual health. In this approach, the close relationship between diet and health is recognized, and seeks to provide an optimal balance of nutrients to strengthen the immune system and promote overall health.

One of the main advantages of holistic eating is its ability to address allergies and food sensitivities at the root of the problem. Rather than simply treating symptoms, such as itching or digestive discomfort, holistic eating focuses on identifying and eliminating trigger foods, promoting healing from within.

The first step in implementing holistic nutrition in times of allergies and sensitivities is to carry out a thorough evaluation of your pet's current diet. Look closely at the ingredients in the foods you eat and keep a record of any allergic reactions or adverse symptoms that may occur. This will help identify potential trigger foods and make it easier to design a new diet more suitable for your furry companion.

Once you've identified problem foods, it's important to completely eliminate them from your pet's diet. This can take time and patience, especially if these are ingredients that are present in most commercial pet foods. Consider consulting a veterinarian or animal nutrition specialist for advice on what foods to replace and how to provide balanced nutrition without compromising your pet's health.

Holistic nutrition also focuses on the quality of the ingredients used. Opting for organic and natural foods can reduce your pet's exposure to additives and chemicals that could trigger allergies or sensitivities. Also, make sure your food is fresh and varied, to provide a wide range of essential nutrients.

Another important consideration in holistic eating is the use of natural supplements that can help strengthen the immune system and reduce inflammation. For example, some pet owners have found benefits by incorporating omega-3 fatty acids into the diet of their furry companions, as these can have anti-inflammatory properties and improve skin and coat health.

In short, holistic feeding is presented as a natural and effective alternative to alleviate allergies and food sensitivities in pets. This comprehensive approach is based on identifying and eliminating trigger foods, as well as providing balanced, quality nutrition. Implementing changes to your pet's diet can take time and effort, but the results will pay off as you see your furry companion enjoy a healthier, happier life.

Once you've done a thorough evaluation of your pet's diet and identified problem foods, you're ready to make the necessary changes to their diet. Below, I'll provide you with some guidelines for implementing a holistic diet to help alleviate allergies and food sensitivities in your pet.

First, it's important to look for healthy and safe alternatives to trigger foods. You can choose commercial foods that are specifically formulated for pets with food allergies or sensitivities. These products are usually free of common ingredients that cause problems, such as chicken, wheat, or dairy. Also, make sure these foods are formulated to provide balanced and complete nutrition for your pet.

If you prefer to prepare your pet's food at home, you must ensure that their diet is complete and balanced. This means including a variety of foods that contain the essential nutrients your pet needs to stay healthy. Remember that it's important to see a veterinarian or an animal nutrition specialist for guidance and to make sure your pet is getting adequate nutrition.

In addition to modifying your pet's diet, you can also consider incorporating natural supplements to help alleviate allergies and food sensitivities. There are several options available on the market, such as probiotics, digestive enzymes and antioxidants, that can help strengthen your pet's immune system and reduce inflammation.

However, it's important to note that supplements should not be used as a substitute for a balanced diet. It's always recommended to talk to an animal health professional before adding any supplement to your pet's diet, to make sure it's safe and beneficial for your pet.

In addition to diet, there are other aspects to consider when it comes to allergies and food sensitivities in pets. For example, it's important to keep an environment clean and free of allergens, such as dust or mites. It is also recommended to avoid contact with other animals or substances that could trigger an allergic reaction in your pet.

Holistic feeding also focuses on your pet's emotional and spiritual health. It's important to provide her with love, attention, and regular exercise to promote her overall well-being. Stress and anxiety can worsen the symptoms of food allergies and sensitivities, so maintaining a calm and relaxed environment for your furry companion is critical.

In conclusion, holistic feeding can be an effective tool for alleviating allergies and food sensitivities in pets. By identifying and eliminating trigger foods, providing balanced, quality nutrition, and considering the use of natural supplements, you can help improve your pet's quality of life and promote their overall well-being.

Remember that every pet is unique and may require an individualized approach to feeding. It's always advisable to seek the advice and guidance of an animal health professional to ensure that you're making the best decisions for the health and happiness of your furry companion.

So don't hesitate to start implementing changes in your pet's diet and see how their quality of life improves. Your dedication and effort will pay off when you see your pet healthy, happy and free from the hassles of allergies and food sensitivities. Your furry companion will thank you!

Chapter 19: Exercise as a Supplement to Holistic Eating

A healthy lifestyle applies not only to us, human beings, but also to our beloved pets. As responsible owners, it's our responsibility to ensure that our pets stay fit and happy. So far, we have explored the importance of a holistic diet for the well-being of our four-legged companions. Now, in this chapter, we are going to discover how regular exercise can enhance the benefits of holistic feeding for our pets.

Exercise is essential for maintaining physical and mental balance in our furry friends. Just like us, pets require adequate physical activity to keep their muscles strong, their weight under control and their energy in balance. When we combine proper nutrition with exercise, we're encouraging a healthy lifestyle for our pets.

But what type of exercise is the most suitable for our pets? Well, that depends on the type of animal and its age. For example, dogs are very energetic animals, so they require a greater amount of exercise compared to cats, which are more prone to being sedentary. However, every pet is unique and requires a personalized exercise routine.

A popular form of exercise for dogs is daily walking. In addition to providing them with the opportunity to socialize with other dogs and people, regular walks allow our furry friends to stretch their paws and let off steam. Let's not forget that our faithful canine companions come from a long line of hunters and runners, so walking is an activity that is deeply rooted in their nature.

In addition to walking, play is another excellent form of exercise for our dogs and cats. Playing is beneficial for both your physical and mental appearance. Interactive toys, balls and scratchers for cats can keep our pets active and stimulated. We can also take advantage of their hunting instinct and hide small prizes or treats around the house for them to look for. This will keep your mind sharp and your legs moving.

Now, if you have a rabbit, a guinea pig, or even a parrot, it's also important to provide them with adequate exercise. Rabbits and guinea pigs can benefit from a race through the garden or a safe space indoors to explore. For their part, parrots require toys that stimulate their mind and controlled flight exercise. Each species has its own needs, so we need to do our research and consult with a professional if we're not sure how to provide them with adequate exercise.

But beyond the physical aspect, exercise also has a significant impact on the emotional well-being of our pets. When doing physical activities, they release endorphins, known as the hormones of happiness, which help them stay in a balanced emotional state. In addition, regular exercise can reduce stress and anxiety, helping them to feel more relaxed and calmer in their daily lives.

In short, regular exercise is an essential complement to holistic nutrition to keep our pets fit and happy. Whether through walks, games or species-specific activities, exercise provides not only physical, but also emotional benefits. In the second part of this chapter, we'll explore how exercise and holistic eating can combine to provide an ideal life for our beloved pets. You'll be amazed at how these two practices complement and strengthen each other. So, keep reading and discover more about this fascinating relationship between exercise and holistic feeding for our pets! In the second part of this chapter, we'll explore how exercise and holistic eating can combine to provide an ideal life for our beloved pets. We've already seen how regular exercise can help keep our pets fit and happy, but now we're going to dive deeper into how this is complemented by proper nutrition.

When we talk about holistic feeding, we refer to providing our pets with a balanced and natural diet that provides them with all the nutrients they need for a healthy life. This involves choosing high-quality foods, without artificial additives or low-quality by-products.

By combining holistic nutrition with regular exercise, we're creating a comprehensive approach to wellness for our pets. Exercise helps them stay physically fit, while a proper diet provides them with the nutrients they need for their development and overall health.

When our pets follow a holistic diet, they are getting the nutrients they need for their physical activity. For example, dogs need a high-protein diet to keep their muscles strong and energy to stay active during walks and games. If we supplement this with regular exercise, we're giving them the chance to burn that energy and maintain a healthy balance.

On the other hand, if our pets don't get enough exercise, they can have problems with weight and lack of muscle tone. This can lead to health problems such as obesity, diabetes, and heart disease. Holistic eating and exercise go hand in hand to prevent and treat these problems.

In addition, exercise and holistic eating can also help our furry companions maintain optimal mental and emotional health. Regular physical activity stimulates your brain, reduces stress and anxiety, and promotes better sleep quality. In addition, an adequate and balanced diet provides them with the nutrients necessary for optimal brain function, which translates into healthier behavior and a better mood.

One way to combine exercise and holistic eating is through eating routines. We can set times for food and exercise, so that our pets can burn energy before or after eating. For example, we can take our dogs out for a walk before their meal so they can exercise and then receive their food as a reward. This provides them with additional motivation to exercise and promotes the formation of healthy habits.

In addition, we can take advantage of the benefits of natural and homemade foods to improve the physical performance of our pets. For example, we can include foods such as lean meat, fresh vegetables and whole grains in their diet to provide them with the nutrients they need for exercise.

There's no single formula that works for all pets, so it's important to adapt nutrition and exercise to the individual needs of each animal. It is always advisable to consult with a veterinarian or an animal nutrition expert for personalized recommendations.

In conclusion, exercise and holistic nutrition are essential elements to keep our pets fit and happy. By combining adequate and balanced nutrition with regular exercise, we are providing our pets with all the tools they need to live full and healthy lives. So, make sure you dedicate time and effort to keeping your pet active and well fed. Your furry companion will thank you!

Chapter 20: Care to consider in holistic nutrition!

olistic feeding is a way of taking care of our pets in a comprehensive way, taking into account all aspects of their health and well-being. In this chapter, we will introduce you to the essential care needed to maintain a successful holistic diet for your beloved furry companion and ensure their long-term well-being.

One of the first things to consider when feeding your pet holistically is choosing the right foods. Instead of opting for processed foods full of additives, we recommend opting for natural, quality foods. Look for those that are made with fresh ingredients and that don't contain animal by-products or artificial preservatives. In addition, it's important to consider your pet's specific needs, such as breed, age, and any medical conditions they have.

Another key point in holistic nutrition is variety. Just like us, pets need a balanced and diverse diet to get all the nutrients they need. Try to include different types of meats, fruits, vegetables and grains in your pet's daily diet. This will help ensure you're getting a wide range of vitamins, minerals, and antioxidants essential to your health.

We cannot fail to mention the importance of hydration in holistic nutrition. Fresh, clean water should always be available for your pet. In addition, you can supplement their hydration with moist or homemade foods, such as soups or broths prepared especially for them. Remember that adequate hydration is key to maintaining your kidney and overall health.

Holistic eating also involves considering balance in the right portions. It's essential to provide your pet with the amount of food needed to maintain a healthy weight. Overeating can lead to obesity, which can lead to long-term health problems. Because every pet is different, we recommend that you consult a veterinarian to determine the exact amount of food your furry companion needs.

In addition to food selection and portion control, it's essential to pay attention to any type of change in your pet's behavior or physical appearance. These changes may indicate that something is not right with your diet or overall health. Keeping an eye out for symptoms such as changes in appetite, weight loss, or dull fur will help you identify any problems and find an appropriate solution.

In short, holistic feeding is a way of caring for our pets from the inside out. Considering the right foods, variety, hydration, balance in portions and being aware of changes in their health are fundamental to providing them with a healthy and happy life. In the second half of this chapter, we will delve into other essential care that you must consider in the holistic nutrition of your pet. Don't miss it!

Once we have reviewed the essential care in the holistic diet of our pets, it is important to highlight other relevant aspects to ensure their well-being and happiness in the long term.

First of all, it is essential to consider the importance of nutritional supplements in holistic nutrition. Although a balanced and varied diet provides most of the nutrients needed by our pets, sometimes it may be necessary to incorporate supplements. For example, some dogs and cats may need omega-3 fatty acid supplements to maintain healthy skin and coats. Others may require glucosamine and chondroitin supplements to care for their joints. It is always advisable to consult a veterinarian to determine what specific supplements may benefit our pet.

Another important aspect of holistic feeding is paying attention to any food intolerances or allergies that our pet may have. Like people, some animals can be sensitive to certain ingredients. If you notice that your pet is experiencing digestive problems, dermatitis, or itching, they may be suffering from a food intolerance. In that case, it's important to identify the problem food and avoid it in your diet. A veterinarian can help you perform allergy tests or recommend dietary changes to control these types of situations.

In addition to food, it is essential to consider other aspects of our pets' lives that may influence their overall well-being. Adequate physical exercise and emotional care are essential to maintaining a healthy and balanced life. Be sure to provide your pet with daily opportunities to move, play and socialize. Not only will this help you maintain your proper weight, it will also contribute to your mental and emotional health.

It is also important to avoid stress in the lives of our pets. Animals can experience stress due to different factors, such as changes in routine, loud noises, or the presence of other animals. Stress can affect the health of our pets and lead to digestive, dermatological and even behavioral problems. If you notice signs of stress in your pet, such as excessive licking, loss of appetite or aggressiveness, it's essential to identify the cause and take the necessary steps to reduce stress in their environment.

Finally, we recommend regular visits to the vet to ensure that your pet is in good overall health. An animal health professional can provide specific guidance on the holistic diet of your furry companion, as well as carry out medical tests and vaccinations necessary to prevent diseases.

In conclusion, the holistic feeding of our pets involves many aspects to consider to ensure their long-term well-being. In addition to proper food choice, variety, hydration, and portion control, it's important to consider nutritional supplements, food intolerances, exercise, emotional care, stress prevention, and regular visits to the vet. By providing a holistic diet and taking care of all these aspects, we will be ensuring a healthy and happy life for our beloved pets.

With these tips, we hope you can start or continue on the path to successful holistic nutrition for your pet. Remember that each animal is unique and may have specific needs, so it's always important to adapt your diet and care to your particular situation. Enjoy the journey of providing your pet with a healthy and happy life through holistic feeding!

Disclaimer

The information provided in this book is for general informational and educational purposes only. The author and publisher make no representation or warranties with respect to the accuracy, applicability, fitness, or completeness of the contents of this book. They are not intended to be a substitute for professional advice, diagnosis, or treatment. The author and publisher shall not be held liable for any loss or damage allegedly arising from any information or suggestions within this book.

By reading this book, you agree that you are solely responsible for your own decisions and actions. If you require specific advice for your personal situation, consult with a qualified professional.

The views expressed by the author do not necessarily reflect the views of the publisher. All information is provided on an as-is basis.

Don't miss out!

Visit the website below and you can sign up to receive emails whenever Gonzalo Estrada publishes a new book. There's no charge and no obligation.

https://books2read.com/r/B-A-OZBBB-OIEZC

BOOKS2READ

Connecting independent readers to independent writers.

Also by Gonzalo Estrada

Self Healing
Visualiza tu Éxito
Cultivando Líderes
Afirmaciones y Empoderamiento
Semillas de Cambio
Cómo convertir TikTok en una máquina de hacer dinero
Cómo hacer dinero con Pinterest
Cómo hacer un ensayo
Cómo Pedir un Aumento de Sueldo
Currículo Poderoso
Entrenamiento sin Violencia
Entrevista Laboral
Gana Dinero con X (Twitter)
Ganar Masa Muscular
Volver a Empezar; el arte de reinventarse
Analiza Resuelve Ejecuta
Holistic Feeding
The ABC of educating your Pet
The Art of Cosmic Connection